BUSINESS STRATEGY:

12 Steps

To Business Sanity

What You Need to Know NOW
to Optimise Your Profits and Your Time,
Grow Your Business and Get Your Life Back
Too !

12 STEPS TO BUSINESS SANITY

Published by Dreamstone Publishing 2010, 2013 and 2014

ISBN: 0958796890

ISBN-13: 978-0-9587968-9-7

If you would like to provide feedback on this book please send it to
info@digitalwordpress.com

Look out for Other Books in the "Business Strategy" Series, coming soon

The next book will be –

5 Steps to Staffing Sanity

What YOU Need to Know NOW

to Optimize Your Profits Through People –

Retain and Develop Good Staff for Small Business

Thank You For Buying This Book !

I hope that you enjoy it and that your Business, and your Personal life, benefit from it!

If you are happy with this information, please be kind and review this book on Amazon.

KIM LAMBERT

DISCLAIMER

The contents of this manual reflect the author's views acquired through her experience on the topic under discussion.

The author or publisher disclaims any personal loss or liability caused by the utilization of any information presented herein. The author is not engaged in rendering any legal or professional advice. The services of a professional person are recommended if legal advice or assistance is needed.

While the sources mentioned herein are assumed to be reliable at the time of writing, the author and publisher, or their affiliates are not responsible for their activities. From time to time, sources may terminate or move and prices may change without notice. Sources can only be confirmed reliable at the time of original publication of this manual.

This manual is a guide only and, as such, should be considered solely for basic information. Earnings or profits derived from participating in the following program are entirely generated by the ambitions, motivation, desires, and abilities of the individual reader.

No part of this manual may be altered, copied, or distributed, without prior written permission of the author or publisher. All product names, logos, and trademarks are property of their respective owners who have not necessarily endorsed, sponsored, or approved this publication.

Text and images available over the internet and used in this manual may be subject to intellectual rights and may not be copied from this manual.

Table of Contents

DREAMSTONE

What Readers are Saying About this Book

"An extremely useful, practical manual to help you streamline and maximise efficiency and profitability of your business. As the author points out at the beginning, many people in small to medium-sized businesses are there because they are enthusiasts and/or skilled in a particular area. They may not understand the dynamics of business itself, and with growing success risk becoming overwhelmed by the myriad demands they now face. This book presents clear insights and guidance to optimizing your business, reducing stress and unnecessary effort, making your enterprise more efficient, more successful and ultimately more enjoyable. Clearly presented, it's solid, workable advice that anyone in business can benefit from." – Bilioph88

"This book gives you perspective on what the important parts of your business really are. It places values on your time, other people's time, your customers and your actions which really forces you to evaluate on the weaker actions which you should eliminate or minimise and the areas you should be focussed on. It shows the value of outsourcing and how to allocate resources. This book is a succinct, well thought guide to better business management. I'm glad I picked it up." Allrandom 32

"Great book for both beginners and advanced business owners. Especially loved the chapter on Personal Time Value. As a business consultant I find that it is a common problem for business owners to undervalue themselves and their services. This chapter gave a very simple and straight forward way to determine if your services are under valued. A simple read with many helpful items for the business owner." Rob Kosberg

Acknowledgements

Thanks to all those business people with whom I have worked over many years, whose personal and business experiences have provided the solid base from which the methodology described in this book has been developed.

Preface

Enjoy Using This Book !

This book is designed to make it easy to tackle a challenging problem – getting clarity about where you are in your business – and to take a structured, step by step approach to changing things to suit your long term aims. It specifically encourages you to work through the steps, in your own time, and completely restructure your business results in the process.

You will end up with more PROFIT, more time for you, and a more valuable business as well as happier employees.

Introduction - Understand Your Business to Optimise Your Profits, and Your Time! - The 12 Steps to Business Sanity

The aim of this methodology is to capture a clear picture of where the best value is

1. For your business, and
2. For you, personally

in spending your time (and the time of your staff).

Once you know that, you have a clear path to increased profits, and reduced stress.

Why is this needed ?

Many advisors talk about systemising and automating your business, about streamlining things and getting the most out of things – this is great and very necessary, but there is a step that comes first – **understanding** what happens in your business well enough to have the information necessary to make the decisions that you need to make, to see **where** you might make those changes to best benefit.

Most people in small business are there because they have an interest in that industry, or skills in a specific area – they have not been taught about business, or how to understand the dynamics of what goes on in their business – they do many things based on "just knowing" what to do.

That great when you start out, but rapidly becomes less and less effective – and suddenly you are feeling "where did my life go ?" as just keeping things afloat swallows all of your time without you understanding why.

That is when a new level of understanding becomes necessary, because :

- It is very easy to do the things that are easy for you, first, rather than the things that will deliver the best result for you, first.
- It is very easy to be driven by the customer who yells loudest, or whom you know best, rather than the one who delivers the most value to your business, either in $ or in indirect value like good PR or list sharing.
- It is very easy to get trapped in the minutiae of your work, because you know exactly how to do it, rather than outsourcing the things that need to be done, but really don't need you personally to do them.
- It is very easy to let the value that you put on something obscure the value that others may put on something (it doesn't matter how short a time it takes you to do a thing, if someone else has no clue how to do it, they will place a high value on getting it done for them) and therefore to undersell your intangible assets.
- It is easy to get to the end of the day and wonder where it went, with many of the "important" things that "should have been done" not completed.
- If you do not understand the value of your time, your individual customers, and the services that you provide, in a detailed and quantifiable way, you cannot plan for, manage, or predict cashflow, or "personal sanity time" availability. (and the two are NOT mutually exclusive)

So – What do you do to get out of these traps?

To avoid the traps listed above, there are a number of steps to take.

This 12 Step program is designed to fill that gap of understanding – to teach you how to assess and understand your business – where your time goes, and the impact of the choices you make about how to do things.

Whilst achieving that understanding may seem difficult at first, it is not hard to do, so long as you work through the steps in order.

This Program will give you the information that you need, to make your own best decisions:

- for you,
- for your business and
- for your profits.

You Take the 12 Steps to Business Sanity

In Summary, the Steps are as follows:

1.   Your Customers

Categorise your customers – use a clear scale (like ad hoc, bronze, silver, gold, platinum for example) – understand who fits where and why – higher graded customers will have an ongoing commitment with you, will be those who bring repeatable, predictable, guaranteed income through your door, or whose publicity value is great enough to be worth supporting regardless of the actual immediate $ that they represent.

2. Your Services Products

Categorise the services that you provide – understand these services as repeatable products, not as "fluffy" variable concepts.

Define a Service catalogue and a price book of your services based on a known cost, margin and therefore % gross profit for each.

To do this for a service that can take a varying length of time, or effort, you will need to look at the average time and effort across multiple instances of providing that service – you want to know the result over many, so that a small loss on one will always be balanced by small or large gains on others.

You will need to get away from a time and materials way of thinking as much as possible.

This is about the perceived value to the customer of the end result that you deliver.

Having them know how long it took can actually undermine its value and how they then report that value to others.

Understand what procedures and systemisations you already have for these services (if any)

3. Your Service Product Groupings

Understand the dependencies between the services that you offer - are some only possible if the client has already purchased another service ? do they fall neatly into "packages of services" ?

Document these dependencies and work packages and produce costs that are based on those synergies (and later marketing material that leverages those patterns)

4. Your Effort Costs

Look at your price book and categorise the tasks based on ease of doing (regardless of who does them) and the time it takes to do them (an average across an expert doing them or a newbie doing them) compared to $ return (which is based on customer perception of value) – you need a table for you, that clearly shows you which services are the most profitable for your business.

5.   Your Business Volume

Look at your business history and trends and work out the likely volume in a week/month/year of each of your main service types in your price book.

This will allow you to understand if a relatively low profit item has enough volume to still be something to focus on significantly (and try to systemise as much as possible, to up its margin).

6.   Your Personal Time Value

Put a $ value on an hour of your personal time – this should be at the high end of what a consultant in a large company, with the sort of skills you have, would be charged out at – do not undervalue yourself.

How much of your personal time in a day needs to be spent on marketing your business, rather than working in it to keep it stable, or preferably growing ?

7.   Your Allocation Of Tasks

Based on the $ value that you put on your personal time (in step 6), and the amount of time that you have identified tasks as taking, for the $ return identified (in step 4) produce a list of tasks that you personally should never do, because they will take longer than the allowable amount of time for the $ return, to match the value of your personal time.

8.   Your Outsourcing Options

Review how outsourcable those tasks identified in step 7 are, and where you would need to outsource them to bring them in at a profit (allow not just the cost of the outsource contractor, but a 15% add to that for your effort in managing the outsourcer).

When dealing with outsourcing, make an early decision on how much to micro manage – if you are paying someone $5 an hour, and they claim 4 more hours than they work, but deliver a great result, do you care ?

Would it cost you more than $20 (based on the value of your personal time defined earlier) to find out that they had claimed extra?

If it would, then the risk based, business value driven answer is – let them claim the extra, you still got a good deal.

Remember – someone does not have to be sitting on a seat in front of you (literally or virtually) to be doing real work on your behalf (sometimes thinking is valid work) nor does the fact that they are sitting there mean that they are doing work – people can slack off as easily in front of you as somewhere else.

9.   Your Critical Cash flow

Understand how many $ per day, gross, your business needs to bring in to cover your operating costs and a reasonable profit/payment to you.

How many of your standard, most common items in the price book have to happen to meet that number ?

This may point out to you that you are under-pricing yourself/your services

10.   Your Customers Value To You

Do your high grade clients already provide you with an income stream that covers the minimum required (as identified in step 9)?

How much of how many people's time, at what total cost, does it take to support them ? Is that really profitable ? or does it need to be streamlined ?

11.   Your Scalability

What common services do you have demand for and capacity to deliver, after supporting those high grade customers ?

Can you ramp up that capacity cost effectively ?

Do you want to ?

12.   Your Business Sanity Plan

Map out a personal activity plan for yourself, and each worker in your business, based on the time values, effort costs and $ returns that you have identified in this process.

No worker should do a task where the return will be less than the cost (sounds simple, but we all fall into that trap at some point).

Review this every month to start with and move that out to three monthly as your confidence in your understanding of the dynamics of your business grows.

OK – But How do I do those steps ???

The best approach is to work through the steps, using the workbook, although you can also do this just using the information in this book (the full manual and workbook is available from www.business2live.com and will soon be released, on Amazon, as both paperbacks and a series of kindle books based around each step). It is important to do this in order, as earlier steps support decisions and conclusions that will be needed in later steps.

You can do this by yourself, but it is best done with someone else acting as a facilitator – they will see things, and ask questions, that would not occur to you, as you are likely to be too close to your business and too deeply entrenched in assumptions about how things work.

You can do this with a friend, a mentor if you have one, or keep an eye out for the soon to be available Business 2 Live online programs with e-lessons that step you through the entire process, personal mentoring and support in addition to all of the materials and lessons.

The next part of this book explains its structure, and how to use it as a guide when working through the steps.

The Structure of This Book

How to Use this Book

This book is broken down into the 12 Steps to Business Sanity. For each Step there are two parts :

Part 1)   **Questions.**

A section, listing the Questions that you will be asked to think about to understand the concepts and areas of your business discussed in that Step

Part 2)   **Actions.**

A section, listing the actions that you will then take, to get clarity about the areas of your business discussed in that Step.

Take notes as you work through the Steps and put them in a folder so that you can easily look back at what you have written in the previous steps.

This will build into a reference for you, that you will look at again and again over the next year, as you apply what you learn here to how your business operates.

The information assessed and considered in each Step feeds into the following steps to allow you to progressively build up your understanding of your business, and adjust your early assessments as the later information gives you new perspectives on it.

It is important to seriously consider the questions for each step and answer them honestly – even if the answers are not what you expect or "think they should be" – this is about getting past assumptions and habits and seeing clearly what is happening, so that you can make valid, good judgements based on a real understanding of what is happening in your business.

Take your time with this, especially if you are doing this process by yourself.

It is critical that you thoroughly understand each step and the information that it gives you, before moving on to the next one.

It is important to write as much as you can/feel you need to, to capture your thoughts and insights as you go.

Things written down will not be forgotten as other information presses in on you.

Please note that a large amount of the information in this book is presented concisely, in bulleted lists to ensure that the steps are kept as simple as possible, and as easy to action.

Chapter 1
Step 1. - YOUR CUSTOMERS

Part 1) - Questions

Answer these questions:

- Who are your customers ?
- Do you already have formally defined levels (eg, bronze, silver, gold etc) for them ?
- If so, what are they?
- What $ results do those levels translate to?
- Are those levels relevant to your market segment ? or should they be adjusted ? (consider what other businesses in your market segment do – how well does this relate?)
- If not, what levels can you create?
- Are any of your customers significant for publicity value more than income streams ?
- If so, who, and why?
- How much effort does it take to support them ? (do you really get the value back in the PR for what you put in? Can you optimise that ?)
- What percentage of your customers are at each level ?

Part 2) – Actions:

- Make a list of your customers, sorted by levels (either the levels that you already have, or new ones that you have decided to use, based on your answers)
- Clearly identify which customers are the best $ return and which are the best publicity return – note which are high on both scales
- Note which customers are LOW on both scales and consider if that result can be improved (make some quick ideas notes if you think they can) or if they are customers you should not have at all.

Customers with the highest combined rating are worth the most to your business in the long term, even if they are not the highest $ return initially.

Chapter 2
Step 2 - YOUR SERVICES AND OR PRODUCTS

Part 1) - Questions

Answer these questions:

- What services do you provide ? (do you actually have any written definitions of them ?)

- Do you already have a services catalogue or a price book of any kind?

- Can you easily 'productise' your services (ie, define them as repeatable, items at a standard cost) ?

- If yes, have you done so ?

- If you think no, why not ? What limits your ability to do so?

- Are your current pricings time and material based ? or deliverable outcome based ?

- Do you understand how long it actually takes/what the input costs are for each item?

- Do you understand what others in the market area charge for something similar ? (and do you have any idea how they derive their pricing ?)

- Do you review your pricing on a quarterly basis and adjust it if appropriate? Do you know what signs indicate that it is time to adjust your pricing ?

- Have you price tested your market (ie priced up steadily to the point where demand levels out)?

- What procedures do you have documented for each service ?

- Are those procedures well enough written for someone who is not expert to perform the work ?

- Are these services systemised or automated in any way?

- Do you understand what makes a customer think that one of your services, as delivered is "good value" or "bad value" ?

- Do you have a unique point of difference that improves your customers perception of value?

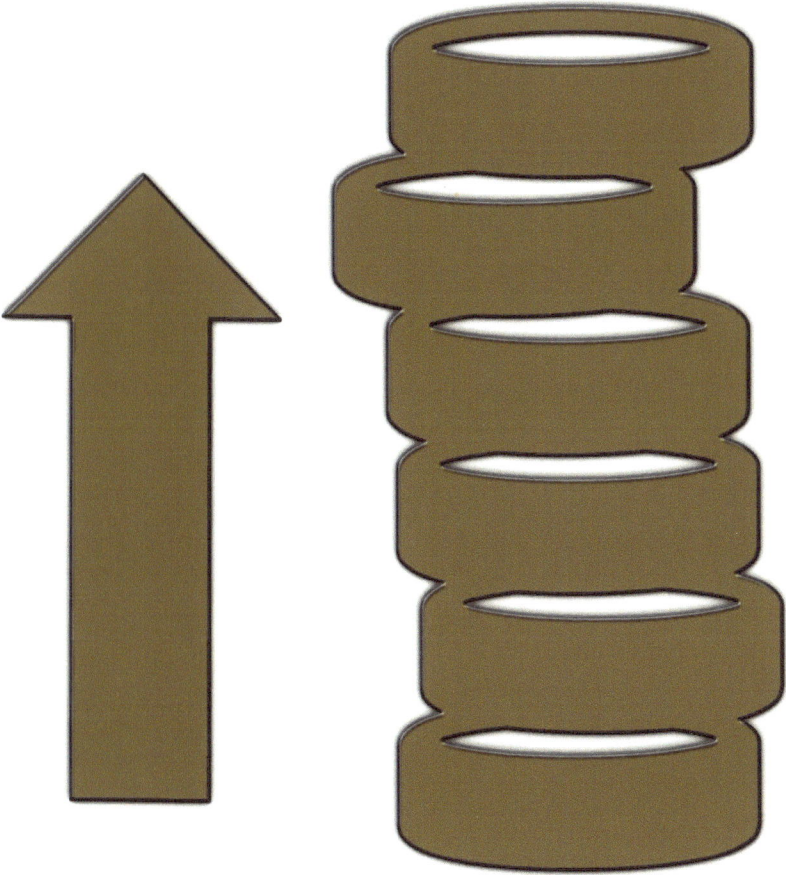

Part 2) – Actions:

- Produce a list of all of the services that you provide.
- Make an initial price decision on what you should charge for each (not what you currently charge, but what you most likely should charge, based on what the customer perceives as good value)
- Then :
    - For each service/product, note any input costs (apart from labour) that exist
    - For each service, note the average hours of labour involved (AVERAGE – not just expert)
    - For each service note the skill level required for a person to do it (and the likely $ per hour cost of such a person)
    - Do the math – for each service, based on the labour and input costs you just identified, are you charging enough ? (you should aim for a gross margin of between 40 and 100% on cost)

Adjust the initial price decisions you made above, based on the margin assessment, until you have found the minimum amount that you should be charging for each service or item.

How different is this from what you charge now ?

How much of a surprise is that ?

- Based on your knowledge of your competitors, is this new price potentially too high? To get some clarity on this you need to assess the following:
    - Does your unique point of difference justify that price level? (give this a rating of 1 to 10 where 10 is "yes, it absolutely justifies it")
    - For each service, give a rating for the existence, and level of detail/quality, of procedures doco (make notes on which can be improved and how fast that can be done)

The items / services with the highest combined ratings are the ones where you have the best opportunity to improve your ability to deliver them effectively, just from improving the procedures

- o For each service give a rating of the level to which it is systemised/automated (make notes on which can be improved and how fast that can be done)

The items / services with the highest ratings are the ones where you have the best opportunity to improve your ability to deliver them effectively, just from improving the systemisation and / or automation.

- o Would the opportunities for improvement in procedures and systemisation that you have identified allow you to reduce the price to a more competitive one? Or could you leave the price as is and make more margin?

- o Add the combined ratings for possible procedures improvement and possible systemisation/ automation improvement to get the **Business Optimisation Potential Score** that indicates how much overall scope there is to optimise your delivery
- Give each service a "perceived value rating" (between 1 and 5) based on previous customer feedback about these service types
- Which of the items with the highest levels of perceived value by the customers are high margin, and highly systemised/ systemizable/ optimizable ? These are the areas to focus on immediately for **boosting profits.**

The higher the Business Optimization Potential score is, the more likely it is that you will be able to reduce (or increase) the selling price or increase the margin that you make.

Increasing the margin should always be the preferred choice, unless there is good business reason to drop the price.

Each time you implement an optimisation, make a new version of your list with updated pricing, cost and margin information.

This list is your Price Book master.

You use this to manage your ongoing awareness of the costs and profitability of the different services that you deliver.

From this list, you can make versions that are just about the services and their descriptions, and their prices, that you might use to give to your customers, but your version, with all of the cost detail and margin information will become very important as we work through this process and will help you make future decisions about your business.

This list (without the prices) is also the basis of your Service Catalogue

(which at this stage will not change, but may do so at later Steps in this process).

Chapter 3
Step 3 - YOUR SERVICE PRODUCT GROUPINGS

Part 1) - Questions

Answer these questions:

- Do you have an existing listing of relationships between different services that you offer ?

- Are any of the services able to be broken down into subsets ? (eg, for a website business, "set up blog", will contain a section called "apply theme and configure theme specific items" which will probably have multiple levels of options – from simple to more complex ones)

- Are any of the services already "bundled" (whether you have previously seen it as that or not)

- Do any of the services have an absolute dependency on others ? (ie cannot be delivered if the other service is not delivered first)

- Do customers often ask for common combinations of services? And if so, do you have a list of exactly what goes into each of the most common combinations ?
- Does bundling services produce an exponential increase in perceived value, or a linear one ?
- Do you already price accordingly for that ?

Part 2) – Actions:

- Looking at your final list of services created in Step 2, see if there are any that immediately can be linked as one being dependent on the other
- Make a list of any "bundles" of services that you have already defined – are there any new bundles you could add to that ? (especially where a dependency exists)
- Does your list of bundles cover all of the common customer requested combinations?
- **If not, keep adding until it does**

- Does the dependency situation, or the bundling, actually make the opportunities for systemisation and automation (as identified in step 2) increase ?

- Give each bundle a customer "perceived value" rating (as you did for the services in step 2). Consider the relationship of these to the values of the individual services as assessed in step 2 – is the value of the whole greater than the sum of the parts ?

- Review the pricing list that you made in step 2 in the light of these values and adjust accordingly

- Highlight any specific aspects that will make good marketing material, based on the customer perceived value assessment.

The higher the Customer Perceived Value, and Marketing Potential, the Bundle has, the more positive impact that Bundle can have on your cash flow and margin, and the more strongly you should consider raising the price.

Chapter 4
Step 4 - YOUR EFFORT COSTS -

Part 1) - Questions

Answer these questions:

- Do you understand which tasks are actually easiest to do ? Not just for you, but for anyone – ie, if you do 3 tasks, and a complete newbie does the same three tasks, will the one that is quickest for you, be the one that is quickest for them – even if they take twice as long to do it as you do? Or are there tasks that are simple, "easy" but tedious, repetitive and do not get quicker no matter how much experience you have?

- Do you understand what level of skill is actually required to do each task/deliver each service to an acceptable level? (no perfectionism is allowed – 80/20 rule applies – the customer will not notice the tiny thing that drives you crazy but costs a ludicrous amount of time to change)

- Do you know what the $ cost is for each skill level (in your hometown, or by virtual workers elsewhere)?
- Do you know what the average time taken is for every service (remember AVERAGE – whether you do it, or a complete newbie does it, using the procedures, if it gets done 100 times, what will be the average time?)

Part 2) – Actions:

- Give each of the services in your price book (the most recent version, including bundles as at Step 3) a rating for ease of doing it
- Give each of the services in your price book a rating for time taken to do it
- Give each of the services in your price book a rating for which skill level is required to do it

Add those three ratings

The higher that number the better value that service is to your business in terms of effort cost, because that means that it takes less time, from a less skilled person and is easier to do overall.

- Review your prices based on these to make sure that your predicted margin is real (based on an average hourly cost for a person to do the work – later steps will go into more detail about actual costs of people effort)
- Review your assessment (done in Step 2) of which items are highest margin and most systemizable/ optimizable and see how they map onto these ratings -

Something highly systemizable will become easier to get done, and be able to be done by a person of lesser skill, once it is systemised.

This will reduce the effort cost score even more, making that service able to deliver even more for your business.

- Will any of the ratings you have made in this step change dramatically if you implement the improvements suggested by your step 2 analysis?
- Make a list of the services which now appear to be most profitable to your business after the analysis done in the steps so far

Does the list surprise you?

If so, consider carefully why, and what assumptions you have been making

Chapter 5
Step 5 - YOUR BUSINESS VOLUME

Part 1) - Questions

Answer these questions:

- Over the last few years (or from the start of your business if you have not been operating long) has there been a consistent pattern to the type of pieces of work that you do ?
  - Is that pattern seasonal ?
  - Is the pattern about types of work (ie, always more of one type of job, consistently over time)
  - Is there a steady increase in numbers of sales over time ?
    - For all products ?
    - Or only for specific products or services ?

- Looking at the items in your price book (as identified in Step 2 and refined in steps 3 and 4) do the trends and patterns, that you have just identified, align with specific services ?

- Are most of your larger volume items your higher or lower priced services/items ?

- Are most of your larger volume items your higher or lower margin items ?

- Are the services which you sell the highest volumes of the ones which you have most systemised the delivery of ? or the least systemised ?

- Do you know how many of each service/item you sell, on AVERAGE, each week/month/year ?

- Are the things you sell most of, the things that you personally most like doing/delivering?

- Are the things you sell most of, the things that are easiest, or hardest to do/make/deliver ?

- Are the things that you sell most of, the things that you personally believe deliver the most value to your customer ? or not ?

Part 2) – Actions:

- Make a graph or table for each of the items from your price book, showing the sales volumes, and the margin percentages over time (weekly if you have not been operating long. Monthly if you have been operating some years)

- If you don't have too many items, make a single graph with lines for each product on it.

Does what you see surprise you ?

If so, what assumptions were you making that do not appear to be true now that you see it graphically?

- Look at the list you made at the end of Step 4, of the items/services which seemed to be most profitable for your business, based on the analysis to that point – does that analysis still hold, when you look at the trends and margin volume over time ?
- Make a table of your price book items in order of how systemised they are now, with a note about how that order may change if you implement the improvements identified in earlier steps.
- Add a column where you record, for each of those items/services which are highest margin now,
- Then add a column to record which are increasing/decreasing in margin over time,
- Then add a column for which are highest sales volume now, and
- Then add a column for which are increasing/decreasing in sales volume over time

Items/services which are increasing in margin <u>and</u> increasing in sales volume and have been identified as further systemizable/ automatable are those that should be your immediate area of focus .

<u>They will return more $ to your business for your effort faster than any others and free up your time in the process</u>

Items which have a high, and increasing sales volume, but not a high margin, may still be worthy of immediate focus.

<u>This is true only if they are also items identified as being easily further automated or systemised</u>

Because doing that will increase their margin, and the volume means that you already know that the demand is there.

- In your table, mark in the final column the order in which the items/services in your price book deserve your focus, based on the above analysis.

Chapter 6
Step 6 - YOUR PERSONAL TIME VALUE

Part 1) - Questions

Answer these questions:

- Do you know what your personal time is worth to someone else ?

- If you were working as a consultant, working for a large consulting firm, what would they pay you per hour? What would they charge you out at per hour to their clients ? (hint, they usually charge someone out at approx 4 to 5 times per hour what they pay that person, as the charge out has to cover overheads and profit as well as base costs) Estimate at the high end of the range – do not undervalue yourself!

- Would the clients of a large consulting firm, paying that $ for you, believe that they were getting value for their money ?
- Do you charge you clients anywhere near that much per hour for your time ?
- If not, why not?

Does the idea of charging that much for an hour of your personal time scare you?

- Consider your clients attitude – do they see what you do as good value for what you charge now ? Would most of them stay if your prices went up tomorrow ? (and would the ones who left be the ones who are most hassle for least result now??)
- Are you the one who does most of the marketing/selling for your business ?

- Are you also the one who does most of the doing ?

- How many hours of each week do you currently need to spend, of your personal time, on marketing your business, to keep it stable, or preferably growing ?

- How many hours per week do you need to spend, of your personal time, doing the "doing" in your business to deliver to your clients as promised ?

- Do you struggle to dedicate that time to marketing, because you are too busy doing ? or because you enjoy the doing more ?

Think carefully about that last answer – it will help you understand your own motivations, and challenges.

Part 2) – Actions:

- Divide a sheet of paper into 4 quarters.
- In the top left box write down the $ per hour that you pay yourself now,
- In the bottom left box, write down the $ per hour that you charge your customers for your time now (either exact if you are billing time and materials, or approximately if you are billing per service outcome),
- In the top right box write what a large consulting firm would pay you per hour if you worked for them,
- In the bottom right box write what that large consulting firm would charge their client for an hour of your time.

Have a good hard look at those numbers.

If the ones on the left are not as big as, or bigger than, the ones on the right, then it is almost certain that you are undervaluing, and underselling, yourself and your business.

- Take the number of hours that you identified as needing to be spent per week on marketing to keep your business afloat/growing.
- Multiply that by the $ per hour in the bottom right box. Write down the answers to the following questions:
  - Could you buy someone else's efforts to do your marketing for you, effectively, for that much a week or less ?

  (this would free you up to deal with more doing, for the extra business they will bring in)

  - Could you buy someone else's efforts to do your doing for you, for that much a week or less?

  (this would free you up to market more, producing more work for them to do, and more profit for your business and probably for you to have more free time as well)

- Take the number of hours per week that you identified as needed for doing the "doing" and multiply it by the $ number in the bottom right box. Write down the answers to the following questions:
  - o If you received that much per week for doing that "doing" effort (that you are already doing), would that increase your turnover ? Would it increase your profit ?
  - o Would that amount allow you to pay others to do the doing, or the marketing, for you ?

- Write down a statement about what you have just learnt about your own value.

What are you going to change because of this ?

- Write a single sentence "action statement" – this is a **PROMISE** to yourself, a commitment to what you will do to change as a result of what you have learnt.

Chapter 7
Step 7 - YOUR ALLOCATION OF TASKS

Part 1) - Questions

Answer these questions:

- Do you choose the tasks, in your business, that you personally do, based on how much $ they return for your time, or because you like doing them most ?

- Do you allocate tasks based on the cost of the person doing them compared to what they return ? or just on who is available now ?

- Do you know how much each person in your business costs (including an allowance for overheads) per hour ?

Part 2) – Actions:

- Look at the lists you created in Step 4, where you identified the time taken for each service/item and the profitability for each service/item. How many $ (just raw, gross income) does each task return, for each hour taken to do it ?
- Compare that $ amount to the $ per hour in the right hand bottom box of your sheet from Step 6 -:
  - Make a list of the services/items where the amount returned per hour is less than that figure from Step 6 –

These are the tasks that you should never do yourself – to do so is to be losing money – your time is worth more than what these tasks will return for it.

○ Make a list of the services/items where the amount returned per hour is substantially more than the figure from Step 6 –

These are the tasks that it is reasonable for you to do yourself, unless you can get someone else to do them for substantially less than your figure from Step 6 (as them doing it for less makes you more profit....)

o Make a list of the services/items where the amount returned is the same as, or only a little bit more than, the figure from Step 6 –

These are the tasks that you can do if you must, but which would be better done by someone else, for a lesser rate per hour than your figure from Step 6

- Look at the ratings that you gave each task in Step 4, for the skill level of the person required to do it. Make a table with a list of the people that you employ (permanent or regular casual), how much they cost per hour, and what skill level they are classified as (descriptions of levels used should match the descriptions of levels you used in Step 4).
- For each person you employ, repeat what you did for you, above, and make the three lists of tasks they should never do, tasks they should only do if no cheaper option and tasks they are best placed to do.

Are there any surprises there ?

Anyone you are paying too much (or maybe too little?)

Anyone you are underutilising?

Are there any tasks that this suggests that no-one you currently have should be doing ?

- Make a list of tasks where it is clear that you urgently need to change who does them.

Chapter 8
Step 8 - YOUR OUTSOURCING OPTIONS

Part 1) - Questions

Answer these questions:

- Do you outsource any tasks now?
  - What sort of tasks ? Only things that you can't do yourself? Or a wider range?
  - How do you decide which tasks to outsource?
  - Do you use offshore/virtual resources? Or only local people physically on site ?
  - Do you understand how much time and effort you actually devote to managing those outsourced resources ? have you costed that into your pricing for tasks that you outsource, when you bill them to your customers?

o Do you regularly review possible sources of outsourcing resources and their costs / or do you just run with the people you already know?

- Do you tend to micro manage your staff ? or not? Are you sure that others see this the way that you do ?
- Do you have trouble believing that someone you can't physically see working, is working?
- Do you tend to fear/believe that staff will try to rip you off if they can ?
- Do you give your staff/outsourcers clear statements of your requirements ?
- Do you trust your staff ? Do you give them work that stretches their skills a little ?
- Do you accept that (for others as much as for yourself) sometimes sitting and thinking something through IS work ? If not – why not ?

Part 2) – Actions:

- Make a list of the tasks that you outsource now.
  - ○ Review what they cost you at an hourly rate – looking at your information from Step 4, are you getting these done cheaply enough ? or do you need to seek a better price ? (or increase the price that you charge your customers for the end result??)

Update your master price book based on this, where required.

- Look at your lists from Step 7, especially the tasks that, based on cost of effort, no-one you currently have should be doing – these are the things that should be outsourced to someone cheaper as soon as possible

- Make a list of the tasks that you need to outsource very rapidly, with a maximum $ per hour rate that you should pay for them. (many outsourcing websites are effectively reverse auctions – people will underbid each other to get your work. Others quote specific hourly rates per person, so that you can clearly see what your cost will be if you know how long the work should take. Others allow you to hire someone on an ongoing basis, full or part time, at very low rates, compared to what it is likely to cost you at home)

Are you uncomfortable with any of those numbers?

Why ?

Think carefully about this.

- Make a list of all of the outsourcing sources/options that you know of. Can you find any more ? Are these the best suited to your needs now?

The industry moves on and new sources come into existence all the time – review this list regularly

- Review your answers to the questions about micro-management and what you believe about work – consider how you will feel about someone on the other side of the world saying "it took me 10 hours" – will you believe them?

Look back at the figure from Step 6 from the bottom right corner of your time value square – this is what your time per hour is worth.

If you are worth $240 per hour and you are paying someone in the Philippines $5 per hour and they claim for 2 hours more than they actually worked, <u>unless it takes you less than 2½ minutes to chase that, it's not worth it</u> – you will spend more chasing it than you will save.

Accept that, so long as they deliver a good result, and their total cost is within the range allowable for you to still make a good margin on the sale to your customer, then you have still got a good deal, even if they have "cheated" you a little – and you have probably made their lives better in the process.

<u>This is a simple, risk based, cost benefit analysis – take the emotion about "being cheated" out of it and look just at cost and value.</u>

- Write a list of your beliefs about work and value from your "staff". Which ones do you want to keep? Which ones are not serving you and should be changed ? Write a list of new beliefs that you will replace the unwanted ones with.

- Research the outsourcing sources that you have listed and identify which ones are best suited to sourcing the work that you need to outsource, as listed above based on your Step 7 analysis

  - For the jobs that you have on now, outsource as many of the related tasks from that list as soon as possible.

  - Keep a detailed record of what happens and use that to both refine your outsourcing choices over the coming months and to help you build, and stick to, your new beliefs.

- Can you apply any of your changes to belief equally to the people who work directly for you, physically here now? Will this make them happier, more loyal and more productive ?

If you have found this step challenging, and it has made you aware of significant changes that you need to make, look out for my book,

5 Steps to Staffing Sanity

What YOU Need to Know NOW
to Optimize Your Profits Through People –
Retain and Develop Good Staff for Small Business,

which is coming soon, to help you resolve that, as it goes into this area in a lot more depth.

Chapter 9
Step 9 - YOUR CRITICAL CASHFLOW

Part 1) - Questions

Answer these questions:

- Do you understand what it costs you to run your business, per day - the basic, committed, unchangeable costs ?

- Have you allowed for power, and a range of other variable, but regular costs in that number ? (stationery, phones, rent, cars, fuel, internet connection etc etc)

- Have you allowed for your Salary in that, as well as the permanent staff you have

- Have you identified how much it would cost, on top of that, per day, to do the extra things that you want to be able to do with the business (extra marketing to grow, new equipment, bigger premises etc)?

- How much do you want to earn yourself ? how much more than you pay yourself now?
- Have you added up what that means in terms of average daily gross cashflow that the business needs to have to deliver what you want ?
- Do you know how many of each of your services/items in your price book it would take to deliver that cash flow per day ?
- Do you know if it is even possible to meet that number, given the items you have, at the prices you have, for how long they take ? Have you considered what to do if it is not?

Part 2) – Actions:

- Make a list of all of your fixed expenses (average out power and phone etc, based on your last few years costs for them) – cost per month, week, day.

- o Double check your numbers and make sure that everything really is on that list.
- o Make sure that your salary is listed at a reasonable rate, not a pittance

Are you surprised by any of these numbers once you see them laid out like this ?

Which ones ?

Are they larger, or smaller than you expected?

- Make a list of your variable/ optional/ discretionary expenses (advertising, training, travel, new product development costs)
  - Double check those and ensure that all of the things that you would like to do are covered.
  - Make sure that increases to your salary are covered here, up to the amount that you would prefer it to be
- From the above, work out the minimum actual and maximum potential cost per day of operating your business
- Looking at your price book, and the analysis that you have done in previous steps about which are your most common items/services sold, work out how many of each service or item you would need to sell a day to make enough cash flow to cover your costs
- Looking at how long each task takes, how many people would you need to do that many, of that task, in 1 day ? Is that more or less than the people that you have ?

This is where the tasks that are most automated/systemized become very important, because they will take less person time to do for their $ return

○ Does any combination of tasks per day meet your minimum required cash flow ? If the answer is no, then you have a problem! (which we will address shortly) If the answer is yes, then you will need to consider what combinations of tasks are likely to provide that cash flow for least effort/cost

○ Does any combination of tasks meet you maximum preferred cash flow ? If the answer is no, then it will be a question of where to focus to improve things. If the answer is yes, then you will need to consider how that combination relates (if at all) to what you do now, and what changes you may need to make, to achieve it.

- Looking at your analysis from previous Steps, see whether the improved systemization or automation options that you have identified will be enough to shift things from not enough cash flow to enough cash flow for the same amount of time expended

- Is the only way to meet your required cash flow through doing a small number of high margin, low effort tasks ?

- Does this analysis suggest that all of your services are still under-priced even after the adjustments that you may have already made?

Chapter 10
Step 10 - YOUR CUSTOMERS VALUE TO YOU

Part 1) - Questions

Answer these questions:

- Who are the customers for the best $ returning tasks identified in Step 9 ? if they are not your platinum and gold level (or whatever you have called your top two levels in Step 1) customers, why not ?

- Are you marketing hardest at selling the services that will most easily cover your costs ? Are you marketing these to the right customer group ?

- Do you know if your high end clients already provide you with enough cash flow, just from them, to support your business ?

- Do you know how much of your cash flow comes from each category of customers ?
- Do you know how much of your cash flow comes from each category of tasks, for those categories of customers ?
- What percentage of your, and your staff's, time does it take to support the high end customers ? is that actually proportionate to the return that you get from them ?
- Do you believe that any group in particular of your customers is not actually profitable for you ?

Part 2) – Actions:

- Write a list of the services that you most want to sell, based on the analysis in Step 9
  - o Identify for each service who the prime customer group/ target market is and how that relates to your customer categories (as developed in Step 1).
  - o Identify whether you already have the marketing material needed to sell this appropriately, or not

- o Write down the first three steps that you can take to sell more of these services
- Write a list of the services that you least want to sell, based on the analysis in Step 9
  - o Identify for each service who the prime customer group is – are they also part of the customer group for the services that you most want to sell? Are they important to your business for other reasons (politics, good word of mouth etc)
  - o Write down what the impact would be, to your business, for each item, if you stopped selling that item (what would it cost you, what would it save you?)
  - o Write down any ideas that you can see, either from the analysis in previous Steps, or new ideas, which would potentially make these services earn more or take less time, or both, to an extent that would make them worth keeping in your price book and service catalogue.

- o Write down the first three steps that you can take to either improve, or get rid of, these services (if you are going to get rid of them, is there someone else who has a business doing those things that you can Joint Venture with, or are willing to refer your customers to?)
- Write a list of items from your price book for which you will increase your price as a result of this analysis
- Write a list of changes that you may make to your customer categorisation, as done in Step 1, based on the picture that this Step has given you of the impact of the preferred service purchases of various groups of your customers in terms of value to your business cash flow
- Write a list of any customer groups/categories who you now believe, as a result of this analysis, to not be profitable for your business to service
  - o Write a list of who you might refer them to
  - o Write a list of any possible options to outsource or subcontract delivery to these people, such that they might then be profitable to you

- Write a list of any ways in which you can streamline your delivery to your most profitable customer group, without them feeling that they receive any lesser level of service

Remember –

The Customer cares about the outcome for them,
the value they perceive it to have,
they DO NOT care about the mechanics of how you achieved it !

Chapter 11
Step 11 - YOUR SCALABILITY

Part 1) - Questions

Answer these questions:

- Do you believe that you have any "spare capacity" in your business which could be used to ramp up your product range, or deliver to more customers?

- Are there any common services that you sell that you believe there is increasing demand for, that you can meet without increasing your costs significantly ?

- Even if you could expand your business to more customers, do you want to ? or would you prefer to expand the range of services which you sell to your existing customers ?

- Is there a point at which ramping up your business will cost you more than it is worth ? Or is there a point at which economies of scale will cut in for some things and mean that things will suddenly get much cheaper to deliver ?
- Does the idea of your business expanding past a certain point scare you ?
- Can you imagine a time when your business would be of such a size that you did little if any of the hands on work ?

Part 2) – Actions:

- From the analysis done in Steps 9 and 10 list services that you will focus on for specific customer categories
- List any of those services which can be ramped up to greater volume (either with those customers, or with others) at little or no extra cost
  - o Make an action list (**no more than 6 steps**) that you will take to make this happen

- List any of those services where a certain volume would have to be achieved for an economy of scale to cut in and make them cost effective
    - Does your current marketing material have the potential to deliver that increase fast enough ?
    - What new ways of marketing those services could you use to get the volume fast enough for the economy of scale to cut in?
- Make a list of your beliefs and fears about what will happen when your business grows past a certain size.
- As you did in Step 8 for your beliefs about staff, identify which of those beliefs you want to keep, and which you want to change.
- Write a list of new beliefs with which you will replace the ones that you do not want to keep.
- Write a description of what your personal day will be like when your business has grown to the point where you do not personally do the hands on stuff every day – how much time will you spend on developing your business ideas and marketing ? How much will you spend purely for yourself ?

- From this scenario, write a job description for yourself, then.

Pin that description up on your wall and consider, each day

WHAT you can do,
in HOW you change your business NOW,
that moves you closer to that result
TODAY.

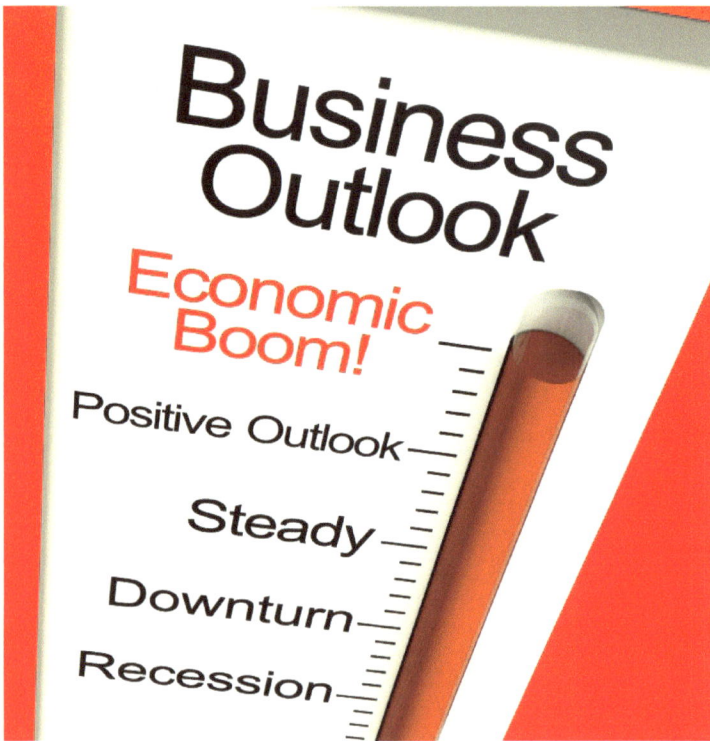

Chapter 12
Step 12 - **YOUR BUSINESS SANITY PLAN**

Part 1) - Questions

Answer these questions:

- Based on the analysis so far do you have any strong ideas about what you personally should, or should not, do each day?
- Have you changed your attitude to your staff management at all ?
- Do you have any existing personal work plans for your staff or yourself?
- Are they still relevant ? If not, what will you change ?
- Do you have an existing business development plan at all?
- Is it still relevant ? If not, what will you change ?

- Do you have existing Joint Venture, affiliate or cross referral arrangements with other businesses ?
- Do you have new ideas for changing or extending those arrangements ?
- Do you have a new picture of the relationship between your customers, your products, your profits and your cash flow ? make some notes about the key things that have changed in how you view that interrelationship

Part 2) – Actions:

- Map out a business goal timeline, which identifies the big things that you want to achieve and an approximate timing for each.
- Write a Business action plan, which takes the first target on your goal timeline and looks at the steps required to get there.
- Go into detail only about the steps that can be taken in the next month.

- Map out for yourself a personal plan which looks at long term goals and the big steps required to get there. Make sure that this is in balance with your business goal plans and will support what you want as well as what the business needs – particularly look at your analysis in Step 9 when considering this.
- Map out a personal action plan which looks at the first goal in the above and maps out the steps that you can take in the next month to move you towards that.

For at least the first few weeks, do a detailed personal work plan and make sure that you do not fall back into doing tasks that are on the "you should never do it" list developed in Step 7.

Commit to looking at this every day, before you start to work.

- Look at the Price Book that you have built, and adjusted, as you have worked through the Steps. Do any final minor adjustments, then print this out and place in a folder that will live on your desk/put it in a document on your phone or Ipad that you will carry with you – this is your reference for every time that you quote on work, and your reminder of what you have agreed, with yourself, that you will charge.

DO NOT be tempted to drift away from it!

- Similarly, look at the services catalogue that you have built up as you have worked through the Steps – This is the full list of services/items that you are offering (including bundled deals) and make sure that you have left nothing out (for now – you can amend this over time, if your offerings change as you optimise your results). Then print this out and place in a folder that will live on your desk/put it in a document on your phone or Ipad that you will carry with you – this is your reference for every time that you quote on work, and your reminder of what you have agreed, with yourself, you will offer as services.

Consider very carefully before you go outside that list – will doing something different really be good for your business? or will it just distract you from the things that are?

- Map out a personal goal plan with each of your permanent or primary staff. Make sure that these are in balance with the business goal plans and will support staff achieving what they want as well as what the business needs – if the staff want to do something that just will not fit, you will need to plan with them to deal with that.

- Map out a personal action plan for each of the staff which looks at the steps they can take in the next month to move both the business requirements and their own goals forward.

- Map out a detailed work plan for each staff member initially, which makes sure that no worker does a task where the return will be less than the cost (using the analysis done in earlier Steps to confirm this) – it seems like a simple thing, but it is easy to lose track and let that happen. These will also drive your ongoing extension of outsourcing those things that cannot be done profitably in house.

- Pin these up where you see them every day and give a copy to each staff member for their own reference – you want them to take responsibility for recognising when they should hand a task to someone else.

- Have a weekly meeting/ virtual meeting/ email based review with all of your staff to track progress. This should start with "what have you completed/achieved this week?"

- Review each of the plans every month and update – map out the next stage of detail, celebrate goals achieved and ensure that they stay live and relevant.

- Once you are more comfortable with the process and the dynamics of your business, you may choose to move this review out to three monthly.

- As your understanding of your business develops, extend your business planning to develop a separate marketing plan, staffing plan etc.

These plans should be approached much the same as the business and personal goal plans that you have just done

– look at what you want to achieve over time, map out the timeline, then tackle things one at a time, focussing always on the next four weeks from where you are now

– small steps will achieve BIG results!

Every 6 to 12 months, go through this whole process again – things will change, markets will shift, you will learn and the answers to these questions will be different.

Each time you do the process, you will "re-optimise" your business, producing increasingly better returns for less effort.

What next ?

Now that you have more time to spend, what will you spend it on?

Some should definitely be spent on you – doing things that you love, with people that you love – after all, we started this whole thing to get you your sanity back!

But some should be spent on building your business further by :

- Developing your ongoing marketing plan
- Developing your ongoing staffing plan – making sure that you always get good staff and that they love working for you, and want to stay
- Building your product or service range with as many products as you can that are minimum cost to develop (combinations of existing material, new spin on existing things, new formats to make things available in, related products etc etc) for maximum margin and perceived value.

- Building your list and making sure that you stay in touch with your existing customer base
- Extending the cash flow sources for your business – getting an offline business online too, for example.
- Making sure that your business is "sale ready", so that you could sell if you wished, get new investors if you wished, immediately, because all of your information would be right there.

There are many programs available to help you do all of these, some from us and some from our affiliated business educators.

If you would like more information on these programs, and to be kept up to date with our new book releases, please sign up for our email newsletters at www.dreamstonepublishing.com .

About the Author

Kim Lambert has extensive business experience in a wide range of areas, from Government and Corporate, to both online and offline small business, wholesale, retail and support services.

She has worked in fields covering everything from Floristry to Information Technology. She owns a number of small businesses currently and is focussing on the areas of Publishing and Photography at present, whilst also progressively translating years of Business experience into this book series.

She has been a speaker at conferences on topics as diverse as Women in Business, and Enterprise, IT and Business Architecture. She holds a Graduate Diploma in Applied Science from Charles Sturt University.

She has previously published business articles in magazines, Travel articles online, cook books (see details later in this book) and photography books (Detailed Beauty – Australia Through The Macro Lens, available on www.Blurb.com, with a new edition due out soon on Amazon, and "The Photographer's Quick Guide to Earning Money From Your Photos", available on Amazon now.)

Should you wish to enquire re articles, speaking engagements or business consultation, she can be contacted through the publisher of this book (info@dreamstone.com.au).

Her current businesses/joint ventures include:

www.business2live.com

www.dreamstone.com.au

www.dreamstonepublishing.com

www.thenotifyservice.com.au

www.dailymacrophoto.com

www.paidtobeme.com (coming soon)

www.dreamstone.photography (coming soon)

Other books in this series will be coming soon!

Look out for the next Book -

5 Steps to Staffing Sanity

What YOU Need to Know NOW

to Optimize Your Profits Through People –

Retain and Develop Good Staff for Small Business

Other Books from Dreamstone Publishing

Dreamstone publishes books in a wide variety of categories. Please visit us at www.dreamstone.com.au – here are some of our other books:-

Get Ranked - The Art of Search Engine Optimisation and Getting Indexed Fast (The Website Success Accelerator Teaches....)

By Charly Leetham

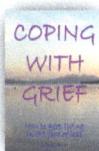

Coping With Grief

By Penny Clements

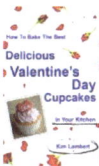

How To Bake the Best Delicious Valentine's Day Cupcakes - in Your Kitchen ("How To Bake the Best.....")

By Kim Lambert

(also available, books for Easter, and Christmas treats)

The Photographer's Quick Guide to Earning Money From Your Photos

By Kim Lambert

95

If you have found this book useful, please give it a positive review on Amazon !

We really do want to know what you think.

Turn Your Small Business Into A BIG Success